GLYNDEBOURNE

A SHORT HISTORY

Michael Kennedy

SHIRE PUBLICATIONS

Published in Great Britain in 2010 by Shire Publications Ltd, Midland House, West Way, Botley, Oxford OX2 0PH, United Kingdom.

44-02 23rd Street, Suite 219, Long Island City, NY 11101, USA.

E-mail: shire@shirebooks.co.uk   www.shirebooks.co.uk

A CIP catalogue record for this book is available from the British Library.

Shire Library no. 621.   ISBN-13: 978 0 74780 821 3

Michael Kennedy has asserted his right under the Copyright, Designs and Patents Act, 1988, to be identified as the author of this book.

Designed by Tony Truscott Designs, Sussex, UK and typeset in Perpetua and Gill Sans.

Printed in China through Worldprint Ltd.

10 11 12 13 14   10 9 8 7 6 5 4 3 2 1

COVER IMAGE
Detail from the 1960 Glyndebourne Festival programme book cover by Osbert Lancaster.

TITLE PAGE IMAGE
The fingerpost in the lane outside Glyndebourne.

CONTENTS PAGE IMAGE
The Organ Room at Glyndebourne, with the new theatre behind, seen from the lawns.

ACKNOWLEDGEMENTS
Artworks and photographs are all copyright the originator and are produced by kind permission of:
BBC Picture Library, page 62 (bottom); BICC, 16 (top); Sue Blane, 46 (top); Peter Brookes, page 51 (top); Cartoon by Mel Calman; © S. & C. Calman, page 41 (bottom); Richard Davies, page 63 (top); Glyndebourne Archive, pages 1, 6, 7 (top), 8, 9, 10, 12 (top), 17, 18, 20 (bottom), 25, 28, 29 (top), 35, 40, 42, 47, 48, 50 (top), 56 (bottom), 58 (bottom), 59 and 62 (top); © Guy Gravett: pages 26, 31, 33, 34, 36, 38, 39 (top and bottom), 41 (top), 43, 45 and 46 (bottom); Clare Hastings: front cover, pages 15, 22 (top), 29 (bottom) and 32; © Mike Hoban, pages 3, 44 (bottom), 35, 46 (bottom) 52 (top and bottom), 53, 54, 56 (top), 57 (bottom), 58 (top), 60 and 64; Richard Hudson, page 51 (right); Edward Reeves, pages 7 (bottom), 12 (bottom), 13 (bottom) and 65; Brigitte Reiffenstuel, page 57 (top); Peter Richardson/Tangerine, page 63 (bottom); Lord Snowdon, page 30; © Sevenarts Ltd, page 44 (top); Sussex Police, page 4; Roger Wood Photographic Collection, © ROH Collections, page 14 (top).

AUTHOR'S NOTE
This is a *short* history of the miracle that is Glyndebourne. Miracle, you say. Well, read the first two chapters. The problem in writing it has been not what to include but what to leave out. I would like to have mentioned many more of the staff past and present, many more of the conductors and singers. I would like to have described more of the productions. I would like to have told more anecdotes, such as Fritz Busch's remark in 1935: 'No stars are ever away at Glyndebourne, because even work is more attractive than the night life of Lewes'. And John Pritchard's quip on hearing that the operatically inexperienced Bernard Haitink was to succeed him as music director: 'I didn't know Brahms had written an opera'. Fortunately Glyndebourne can already boast an impressive bibliography, to which those who wish for more detail can turn. All writers about Glyndebourne are in some way indebted to the authors who have tackled the subject before; and my thanks also go to Sir George Christie, Joanna Townsend, Julia Aries and Helen O'Neill.

M.K.

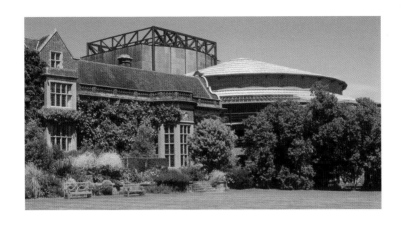

CONTENTS

'DO THE THING PROPERLY'

'GLYNDEBOURNE, an English opera house near Lewes in East Sussex.' This *Dictionary of Music* entry is prosaically accurate but conveys nothing of the special and magical thrill that the name Glyndebourne holds for everyone who has attended opera there since 1934. Opera at Glyndebourne remains a unique experience, to be enjoyed from mid-May to the end of August and for three weeks in the autumn when the touring company occupies the theatre before taking three operas into the regions. There have been many claims that somewhere or other there is a 'second Glyndebourne', but these never prove to be sustainable. What makes Glyndebourne unique is that it remains a family's private home in which one feels more like a guest than a patron. Nowhere else offers international musical standards in such pleasing surroundings – a beautiful estate in the heart of the Sussex Downs, with gardens, lawns, lake, and facilities for dining or picnicking (weather permitting) in the eighty-five-minute interval of the opera. The superb opera house is the second on the site in seventy-five years. What must have seemed to be a madcap folly in 1934 has become a world-famous guarantee of quality.

We owe all this to the money, determination, vision and eccentricity of John Christie and to the professionalism, tact and wisdom of his wife, the soprano Audrey Mildmay. After them came their son George and his wife Mary, who took Glyndebourne into a new era and who have now handed over to their son Augustus (Gus).

There has been a manor house at Glynde Bourne, as it was often spelt, since the fifteenth century and it was owned by the Hay family until the Christies came on the scene in the late eighteenth century (the name was originally Swiss, Christin). John Christie was born in Eggesford, North Devon, on 14 December 1882, the only child of Augustus Langham Christie and Lady Rosamond Wallop, daughter of the fifth Earl of Portsmouth. (Eggesford was her father's house.) Augustus's father William had enlarged and altered many features of the Glyndebourne manor house in accordance with Victorian taste, but John spent his childhood and early youth at Tapeley Park, a Christie property in Devon.

Opposite:
An aerial view of Glyndebourne house and theatre from the south, taken in spring 2004. Glyndebourne house, seen on the left of the site, is dwarfed by the ten-year-old theatre.

He was sent to boarding school when he was six and in 1896 went to Eton where he concentrated on science but was moved into the army class. Although he had no wish to go into the army, he passed into the military academy at Woolwich in 1900 and was relieved when an injury to his foot in a riding accident, which left him slightly lame, enabled him to leave and to pass the entrance examination for Trinity College, Cambridge, to study natural science. Because of his foot and a subsequent injury to an eye, in which he later lost the sight, he was unable to play games, but he loved and later played cricket and became a first-class shot. He developed a keen sense of fun and always found it difficult to keep a straight face when he was pulling someone's leg.

Watercolour of Glyndebourne, *c.* 1756. The original fifteenth-century house is almost hidden behind the imposing addition made by John Hay in the late seventeenth century.

On taking his degree, he returned to Eton in 1906 as an assistant master to teach science. In 1914, on the outbreak of the First World War, he obtained a commission in the King's Royal Rifle Corps and fought in France. In 1916 he was invalided out with the rank of Captain. He was also awarded the Military Cross.

While at Cambridge he had become passionately addicted to the music of Wagner. Dr Charles Harford Lloyd, precentor of Eton since 1892, introduced John to the Munich and Bayreuth festivals. Glyndebourne had become John's principal residence since 1913, but Lloyd was reluctant to retire to Sussex because there was no good organ to play. In 1919 John demolished the unused fives court and a conservatory and built an organ room in their place. Failing to find an organ to suit Dr Lloyd, he bought an organ-building firm and instructed it to install an organ of Lloyd's own design. Lloyd died before the instrument was completed.

John subscribed in full to Hilaire Belloc's dictum that 'it is the business of the wealthy man to give employment to the artisan' and believed that no landowner could be efficient if he did not have practical experience of the work he asked others to do. Ringmer Building Works, the village's garage, forge and electrical repair firm, his hotels and golf courses in Devon, all benefited from his enterprise and knowledge.

He filled Glyndebourne with shooting-party guests who found themselves listening to music performed either by amateurs or sometimes by professionals such as the pianist Myra Hess. On 3 June 1928 the first scene of Act 3 of Wagner's *Die Meistersinger von Nürnberg* was performed in the Organ Room, with the tenor Steuart Wilson as Walther and John Christie as Beckmesser and piano and organ accompaniment. On 5 and 6 January 1929, the choice was Act 1 of Mozart's *Die Entführung aus dem Serail*. A nineteen-piece orchestra was conducted by Arnold Goldsbrough. The cymbals player was John. Two years later the extract was repeated, with the soubrette role of Blonde sung by a member of the Carl Rosa Opera named Audrey Mildmay. She recalled the occasion as hilarious, with comical mishaps all round. She was paid £5. John, now forty-eight and believed by all his

Three generations of the Christie family on the south lawn at Glyndebourne: John Christie as a boy with his father Augustus Langham Christie and, seated, his grandfather William Langham Christie.

Among his many local businesses, John Christie established the Ringmer and District Electric Company, which had a shop in Lewes High Street.

7

Cast list from the 1928 amateur performance of an extract from *Die Meistersinger von Nürnberg* given in the Organ Room at Glyndebourne, featuring John Christie as Beckmesser. His interpretation of this farcical role caused one of the housemaids to be carried from the room in hysterics.

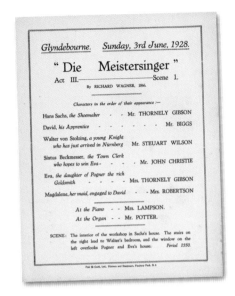

Glyndebourne. Sunday, 3rd June, 1928.

" Die   Meistersinger "

Act III.————————————Scene 1.
By RICHARD WAGNER, 1866.

Characters in the order of their appearance :—

Hans Sachs, *the Shoemaker* - - Mr. THORNELY GIBSON

David, *his Apprentice* - - - - - - Mr. BIGGS

Walter von Stolzing, *a young Knight
who has just arrived in Nürnberg* Mr. STEUART WILSON

Sixtus Beckmesser, *the Town Clerk
who hopes to win Eva* - - - Mr. JOHN CHRISTIE

Eva, *the daughter of Pogner the rich
Goldsmith* - - - - Mrs. THORNELY GIBSON

Magdalene, *her maid, engaged to David* - - Mrs. ROBERTSON

At the Piano - - Mrs. LAMPSON.
At the Organ - - Mr. POTTER.

SCENE: The interior of the workshop in Sachs's house. The stairs on the right lead to Walter's bedroom, and the window on the left overlooks Pogner and Eva's house. *Period* 1550.

Grace Audrey Louisa St. John Mildmay, always known as Audrey, as a young woman.

friends to be a confirmed bachelor, fell head over heels in love with thirty-year-old Audrey. He followed her to wherever the Carl Rosa was playing and regularly sent her Fortnum & Mason hampers because he thought she looked under-fed.

Audrey was born in Herstmonceux, not far from Glyndebourne, on 19 December 1900. Her father was a clergyman and eventually heir to a baronetcy. He moved to become a vicar in British Columbia, where Audrey went to school and began her musical education. She returned to England in 1924 and studied singing at the Webber-Douglas opera school. She then went on a long tour of North America as Polly in *The Beggar's Opera* and on her return joined the Carl Rosa. She and John were married in Somerset on 4 June 1931 and went on honeymoon to Salzburg where Audrey had an operation for appendicitis and John had his tender appendix removed 'to keep her company'. Back at Glyndebourne they discussed plans for building an extension to the Organ Room to hold about one hundred and fifty. This was a time of international financial crisis and John decided it was now or never for his theatre. Trenches had been dug for the foundations when Audrey said at dinner one evening: 'If you're going to spend all that money, John, for God's sake do the thing properly'. This remark changed the whole nature of the scheme. Instead of semi-amateur performances for the tenants and villagers there were to be international

standards. A new site for the theatre was chosen and the building was re-
designed. Late in 1932 Audrey had singing lessons from a young Hungarian,
Jani Strasser, in Vienna. John told him about the opera house and Strasser
suggested Mozart operas as ideal for it. He coached Audrey in the roles of
Susanna in *Le nozze di Figaro* and Zerlina in *Don Giovanni* and subsequently
stayed at Glyndebourne from February to June 1933.

News of the planned festival broke in the *London Evening News* on 29 June
1933 and caused little stir. Compared with today, opera in 1930s England
was not 'news'. Glyndebourne, the paper announced, would be 'the
permanent home of international opera in England'. Built by Captain John
Christie it would open in 1934, with either *Don Giovanni* or – *pace* Strasser
– Wagner's *Die Walküre* and, the reporter quoted Christie, 'in addition to the
Ring we shall produce *Parsifal,* probably at Easter'. If this seemed unlikely,
somehow the rank 'Captain' confirmed it as belonging to the realm of
eccentricity, a lunatic country-house experiment by an enthusiastic but
unpractical rich amateur which would be certain to fail. 'My wife will take
part', the Captain added, intensifying suspicion that this was another
indulgence in the manner of William Randolph Hearst's disastrous promotion
of the singing career of his wife Marion Davies. What the doubters could not
know was that a seriously professional approach was inspiring the project
and some did not seem to know that Audrey was a successful professional
singer. However, before we reach the opening season in 1934, it is time to
recount the building of the house.

John and Audrey
Christie pictured
while on holiday
in Germany.
The dachshund
belonged to their
hostess.

BRICKS AND MORTAR AND ROSES

JOHN CHRISTIE'S first addition to the manor house was the magnificent Organ Room. He took immense interest in the estate, creating a modern feudal system. He created and developed local companies whose employees worked loyally for him all their lives. They could not have foreseen that they would one day appear as 'extras' in Verdi's *Macbeth*! The Organ Room was designed by Edmund Warre and built by John's Ringmer Building Works. The organ was built by Hill, Norman and Beard. The total cost was £18,000, a large sum at the time. The room is eighty feet long, built of red brick and traditional Bath stone with oak panelling, a plaster-work ceiling and mullioned windows inset with coats of arms. As John's interest in opera grew, his interest in organs diminished, and eventually all the organ's functional parts were removed, leaving only the casing.

Work on the theatre, also designed by Warre, began in October 1931 – before official approval had been given. Attached to the Organ Room, it was rectangular with a classical façade facing the lawns and an auditorium with a barrel-vaulted ceiling, which kept out extraneous noise but did not keep out the bats. These added to the atmosphere in some scenes (the cemetery in *Don Giovanni*, for example), but could be startling for singers and audience. There was seating for three hundred, with eleven further seats in a raised box at the back. The sides and rear were oak-panelled and there were three-pronged lighting brackets designed by John himself. Usually accompanied by his pug, he revelled in every aspect of the construction work. His science training came in useful for the lighting and stage effects, which he had studied in European opera houses. With an estate electrician, Norman Thorpe, he designed a lighting switchboard more advanced than any in Britain. He enjoyed obtaining an estimate for some requirement and then using his own workers to provide something better and cheaper. Of course, because of the tight time schedule several things were overlooked. In the first season scenery had to be moved in and out via a single door on to the lawns, dressing-rooms were rudimentary and the orchestra pit was far too small. Over the next few years, with the assistance of the chief stage technician Jock Gough, the stage

Opposite:
The theatre lighting board, 1934. It was designed by John Christie after he had studied models in various European theatres.

11

Construction of the Organ Room in 1919. John Christie actually started planning the Organ Room as early as 1917, and the room replaced an old fives court and a conservatory.

was made deeper, dressing-rooms and a green room were built, capacity was increased to 433 seats, and dining rooms called Over, Middle and Nether Wallop were added, with a covered way so that the audience could walk from the theatre to the restaurants without getting wet. The dining rooms were

The auditorium as it appeared in 1934. John Christie's acoustic adviser was Hope Bagenal, who described Christie as being in the 'category of *mysterium tremendum* rather than that of an ordinary client'.

named after three villages in Hampshire from which the Earls of Portsmouth took their family name, a happy tribute to John's mother. In 1938 he installed a fly-tower. Gough was a strong character and knew how to handle John's volatility, infuriating changes of mind and wilder extravagances.

Despite the onset of war in 1939, plans were made for the 1940 season but were later abandoned. In July 1940, Audrey and their two young children, Rosamond and George, sailed to Canada, where they stayed until May 1944 and had a lean time because strict currency regulations meant that John could not send them much money. Audrey sang in concerts throughout North America, wearing herself out in the process. George remembers being refused a second helping at breakfast with the words: 'Certainly not, we're down to eleven dollars'. Glyndebourne meanwhile was home to one hundred London evacuee children and its rose garden became a vegetable patch. John and Jock Gough

Portrait of the indefatigable Jock Gough, Glyndebourne's first stage foreman. John Christie took over the lease on the Tunbridge Wells Opera House, where Jock worked, in the 1920s, and when John turned his attention to Glyndebourne, Jock came too.

Glyndebourne house, Organ Room and theatre viewed from the south in 1934. The following year Christie added a block containing individual dressing rooms and a green room to his theatre, and in 1938 the distinctive, shingle-clad fly-tower was built.

John and George Christie in the front hall at Glyndebourne.

continued to maintain the theatre, working on the roof and the lighting, but nothing substantial could be done because of wartime shortages of labour and materials and, later, post-war restrictions of many kinds.

A feature of Glyndebourne is its beautiful gardens. Until 1913, when John moved in, there was a single terrace by the house and a small lawn bounded by a dwarf brick wall. A large orchard and kitchen garden area at the back was where the opera house was eventually sited. John's plans for improvements were inevitably ambitious. In 1920 he began sowing new lawns, extending the terrace and growing grapes, nectarines, peaches and tomatoes in his greenhouses. In 1924 he appointed Frank Harvey as head gardener. He was another strong character able to stand up to his employer when necessary. Later Audrey also took a keen interest in the gardens, where the herbaceous borders were outstanding, and was happy to be advised by her mother-in-law. Members of the orchestra

Evacuees raking up leaves at Glyndebourne. Three separate nurseries were established at Glyndebourne for the duration of the war, housing children between two and five years of age from the East End of London.

liked to spend the long dinner interval on the croquet lawn. When, after 1950, picnicking became more popular with the audience, regulars had their favourite spots – near the green room, by the lake, in the Urn Garden or on the ha-ha lawn.

In spite of post-war difficulties, John returned to his passion for improving and expanding the theatre. In 1950 he executed the plans for extending the theatre and enlarging the auditorium to 592 seats by removing his box and adding seats in the balcony. This was done with his characteristic total disregard for rules and regulations. Between 1951 and 1957 when it was particularly difficult to obtain permission for structural work, John engaged his own Ringmer Building Works to widen the auditorium and, to maintain sight-lines, enlarge the proscenium. The barrel-vaulted ceiling was replaced within the existing roof structure but this adversely affected the acoustics.

Audrey Christie died in 1953 at the age of fifty-two after a long and painful illness and her role as brake to John's eccentricities was taken over by Jock Gough, dictatorial as he too could be. Over the course of time, John remained the figurehead but gradually divested himself of the day-to-day running of affairs. In 1958 he handed over the chairmanship of the company to his twenty-four-year-old son George, who had just married Mary Nicholson. The last major addition to the theatre in John's lifetime was the

Osbert Lancaster cartoon of the audience in the auditorium, created for the cover of the Festival programme book in 1969.

Glyndebourne house and theatre during the 1960s.

1959 rehearsal stage, now called the Ebert Room, whereby one opera could be rehearsed or performed on the main stage while at the same time another was on the rehearsal stage.

John Christie died aged seventy-nine on 4 July 1962, shortly before a performance of *Così fan tutte*. His death coincided with the need for financial stringency. Glyndebourne Productions had an increasing deficit because box-office income would no longer cover costs. An appeal was launched in 1964

to help pay for a new lighting control system and for the office accommodation and general maintenance. This raised £64,064 in a year, but the work had cost £93,313. Losses continued in this way until, in the mid-1970s, George Christie initiated a drive for private sponsorship. Several large and generous gifts ensued. In 1984 a fiftieth-birthday appeal was launched to improve backstage facilities and by October 1985 it had raised over £625,000. By this date Glyndebourne's status in the opera world had risen to dizzy heights at a time when opera in Britain was thriving – in addition to the Royal Opera at Covent Garden and English National Opera at the London Coliseum, there were Scottish Opera, Opera North and Welsh National Opera – all subsidised. Glyndebourne was a summer festival and demand for tickets was phenomenal; the box office could barely cope. The only answer to the problem, George Christie realised, was to build a new opera house. He disclosed his plan in the 1987 programme book: 'The idea is merely a glint in my eye ... which could not conceivably materialize in less than half a dozen years, if ever'.

But that is a long way ahead. We must return to 1933.

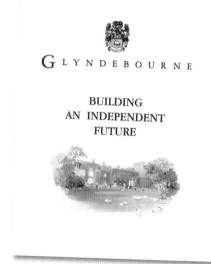

Cover of the rebuild brochure produced in 1987 and featuring artwork by Sir Hugh Casson.

G L Y N D E B O U R N E

BUILDING AN INDEPENDENT FUTURE

The Glyndebourne estate staff and tenants in 1936, outside the Green Room. The Christie family can be seen on the steps behind.

GLYNDEBOURNE
LEWES, SUSSEX

FESTIVAL OPERA HOUSE

FOYER   STAGE

FOR TWO WEEKS
MONDAY, 28 MAY to SUNDAY, 10 JUNE

MOZART FESTIVAL in Italian :

The Original Text

"FIGARO"
"COSI FAN TUTTE"

SUNDAY ORCHESTRAL CONCERTS
Conductor - FRITZ BUSCH
Leader - ADOLF BUSCH

The Orchestra will be led by THE BUSCH QUARTET

Names of International Artists will be announced later

Opera Prices: Box (Seat Nine) 20 gns.   Stalls, £2 0s. 0d., & £1 10s. 0d.

Telephones : **NORTH 3003 (3 lines)** and **RINGMER 28**

DREAM BECOMES REALITY

IN THE SPRING and summer of 1933 life at Glyndebourne was hectic. John Christie, his pug under his arm, supervised and took part in the work on the theatre and Hamish Wilson was designing sets and costumes for the selected operas. By Christmas 1933 it had been decided that the first season would begin on 28 May 1934 with two Mozart operas, *Le nozze di Figaro* (six performances) and *Così fan tutte* (six performances), both to be sung in Italian. Sir Thomas Beecham had been invited to conduct but never replied because he thought the whole idea was preposterous. The violinist Adolf Busch then suggested his brother Fritz to the Christies. Fritz Busch had been *Generalmusikdirektor* of Dresden Opera but had recently left because of his opposition to Nazi policies (he was not Jewish). The Christies subsequently invited Fritz to conduct the first season, but he was dividing his time between Copenhagen and Buenos Aires and at first refused because of prior engagements at the Teatro Colón. But the season there was shortened and in January 1934 he told Glyndebourne he was available (he secretly believed there would never be a second season).

As soon as he arrived, Busch realised what ideal conditions Glyndebourne offered. He needed a first-rate director, a functionary of whose importance Christie was unaware. Busch recruited Carl Ebert from Berlin, another non-Jewish opponent of the Nazis who was anxious to leave Germany. They had worked together on a Mozart opera at Salzburg. As his 'managerial assistant', Busch brought to Glyndebourne Rudolf Bing, an Austrian Jew who had worked with Ebert in Darmstadt until forced to leave Germany for Vienna to resume work as an impresario. He needed little encouragement to join the team in Sussex with responsibility for engaging foreign artists (and he had Jani Strasser to help him as répétiteur). He was appointed General Manager in 1936. Thus Christie's venture benefited from European politics by the bringing together of three men very experienced in the hazardous world of opera who, probably much to their surprise, dedicated themselves to making a success of their extraordinary employer's ideas. He for his part ceded responsibility for all artistic matters to them, provided they discussed them

Opposite:
Poster for the first Glyndebourne Festival Opera season, 1934.

19

John Christie's triumvirate: Rudolf Bing, Fritz Busch and Carl Ebert.

Label used to reserve carriages for members of the Glyndebourne audience on the train from Victoria to Lewes.

SOUTHERN RAILWAY

RESERVED

FOR PATRONS OF

GLYNDEBOURNE OPERA FESTIVAL

PENALTY under Bye-Law 18 for UNAUTHORISED REMOVAL OF THIS LABEL—£5

with him first. There were occasional disagreements, but the plan worked.

Next came assembly of an orchestra. This comprised thirty-three members of the London Symphony Orchestra, including the oboist Evelyn Rothwell – later Lady Barbirolli (sixty years later she attended the opening of the new theatre). Seat prices were fixed. A box for nine cost 20 guineas (the equivalent of £1,080 in 2010), stalls seats ranged from £1-10s (£77 in 2010) to £2 (£103), prices unheard of in England at that time. Even Audrey thought they were outrageous. The weather on 28 May was perfect and the first-night audience of just over one hundred was entranced by the gardens, the food and wines, and the free programmes in gold covers. Many members of the audience were titled and well known in society, such as Lady Diana Cooper. Many had come for 'a lark' and the novelty of the setting. Some came by car (later there was a room for their chauffeurs) and others by train – the 3.10p.m. from Victoria to Lewes. Other travellers were surprised to see passengers in full evening dress at that time of day. Evening dress was 'recommended' by Glyndebourne, never mandatory (John Christie wore white gym shoes on many occasions). To enable people to drive home in good time or to catch the train back to London, performances began and ended much earlier than in London. The music was the thing – there was nowhere else to go and nowhere else to dine except at Glyndebourne.

The remarkable fact is that Glyndebourne's musical reputation was established at the very start. The highest quality singers from both home and abroad were engaged. Critics wrote of the finest *Figaro* ever seen and of 'undisciplined enthusiasm' at the end. Salzburg was not in the running as far as Mozart was concerned, one critic wrote. The bats made a well-timed entrance in the final garden scene. Busch's conducting was praised, as were Ebert's production and Wilson's sets. At a stroke

Members of the audience by the lily pond in the walled garden behind the opera house. In 1937 the pond was filled in and the area was enclosed to create the covered way.

Glyndebourne became a major contender in the world of opera. 'The first performance was as near perfection as anybody has the right to hope for', the *News Chronicle* stated. Probably an exaggeration, for the German-speaking members of the cast had trouble with rapid-fire Italian. But the singing was good – Willi Domgraf-Fassbänder (German) as Figaro, Roy Henderson as Count Almaviva, the Finnish soprano Aulikki Rautawaara as the Countess, Luise Helletsgruber (Austrian) as Cherubino, the British singers Norman

Aulikki Rautawaara as the Countess and Audrey Mildmay as Susanna in the letter scene from *Le nozze di Figaro*, 1934.

Allin (Bartolo), Heddle Nash (Basilio), Constance Willis (Marcellina) and, of course, Audrey Mildmay as Susanna. She had the double task of singing this long and demanding role and of being the hostess at Glyndebourne. She had also given birth to her first child, Rosamond, in October 1933 and on the opening night was two months pregnant. As a recording shows, she was in no way outclassed by the foreign singers. Those who wrote her off as a second-rater with a rich husband were proved wrong. When Busch had auditioned her in March 1934, he wrote that he would have engaged her for Dresden.

Osbert Lancaster cartoon of the Glyndebourne bats making an unscheduled appearance during *Le nozze di Figaro*.

The second opera was *Così fan tutte,* in those days almost a rarity, a fact which accounted for the small audiences. For those who attended, it came as a revelation. Fiordiligi and Dorabella were sung by Ina Souez and Luise Helletsgruber, Ferrando and Guglielmo by Heddle Nash and Willi Domgraf-Fassbänder, Despina by Irene Eisinger and Don Alfonso by Vincenzo Bettoni, the only Italian in the cast. The opera was cut, as it still is too often. It was recorded by HMV, who had also recorded parts of *Figaro.* Apart from teething troubles – which are discussed in detail in longer histories of Glyndebourne – everyone connected with the Festival knew they had a hit on their hands and fell under its spell. 'International opera in Sussex' was no longer a dilettante's boast but a realisation to be taken seriously. Christie lost £7,000 (the equivalent of £360,000 in 2010) – he had expected more – and was sanguine about the empty seats. He had proved that, in the right conditions, opera could be produced in England to as high a standard as anywhere in Europe. The secret, of course, as it still is, was the thorough preparation – singers absorbed and lived their roles.

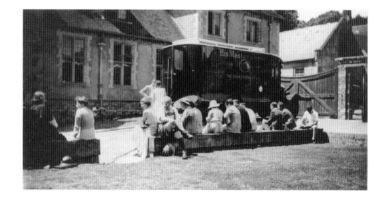

John Christie, dressed in lederhosen, with members of staff and the cast, during a break between recording sessions at Glyndebourne in 1935.

The 1935 season was increased to twenty-five performances of four operas, seven of *Figaro* and five of *Così*, with casts mainly unchanged. Audrey had had a son, George William Langham Christie, on 31 December 1934 and she returned to sing Susanna. The other two operas were *Die Entführung aus dem Serail* and *Die Zauberflöte*. The role of the Mute in *Entführung* was taken by Joseph Childs, the Christies' butler. In 1936 *Don Giovanni* entered the repertory. It was recorded by HMV and Act 1 was broadcast by the BBC. The season totalled thirty-two performances and in Coronation Year, 1937, there were thirty-five of the same five operas between 19 May and 3 July. Illness compelled Audrey to cancel all her performances, but otherwise it was all good news – a profit in 1937 of £2,723, few empty seats and a new restaurant, Wallop Dining Hall, later renamed Middle and Over Wallop.

Christie realised that Glyndebourne had to stage something besides Mozart in 1938. His preferred choice was Donizetti's *Don Pasquale*, with Audrey as Norina. Busch was not keen, but his and Ebert's salaries had just been increased by fifty per cent and they also realised that the financial and artistic freedom allowed them by Christie could be matched nowhere else. Nor was Busch enthusiastic about Ebert's choice of Verdi's *Macbeth* in the 1847 version. It had never been professionally staged in Britain and therefore would win plaudits for enterprise, but it might frighten away the

Kenneth Green painting of *Die Zauberflöte* set, 1935.

Francesco
Valentino in
the title role of
Macbeth, 1938.

Glyndebourne audience, which Ebert classified as seventy per cent 'die Snobs' and thirty per cent music-lovers. In the event it won much prestige. This was also the first Glyndebourne opera to be designed by someone – Caspar Neher – other than the rather amateurish Hamish Wilson. Vera Schwarz sang Lady Macbeth and the title role was a triumph for Francesco Valentino. There were eleven performances out of the season's thirty-six.

Mariano Stabile
as Malatesta, and
Salvatore Baccaloni
as Don Pasquale, in
Glyndebourne's
first non-Mozart
opera, Donizetti's
Don Pasquale, 1938.

The starry cast for *Don Pasquale* had Dino Borgioli as Ernesto, Salvatore Baccaloni as Pasquale and Mariano Stabile as Malatesta. Stabile was the new Figaro in the fifth revival. Because of the uncertain international situation in 1939, no new operas were added. At thirty-eight performances it was the longest season so far. On the last night, in his customary speech, Christie began, 'I have some very serious news.' Dead silence. Was it war? 'For the first time since 1908, Harrow has beaten Eton at Lord's.'

Although plans for 1940 included Bizet's *Carmen*, Busch and Ebert were in America and Turkey respectively and would probably have faced internment if they had returned to Britain. Bing, by now a naturalised British citizen, worked for the John Lewis Partnership, a loyal supporter of Glyndebourne, and in January 1940 he arranged a touring production of *The Beggar's Opera* with Michael Redgrave, Audrey Mildmay and Roy Henderson. When it ended, Audrey went to North America. She sang her last Susanna in Montreal in 1943, under Beecham.

Michael Redgrave and Audrey Mildmay as Macheath and Polly in *The Beggar's Opera*, 1940. Directed by a young John Gielgud, the production was seen in seven different venues on a tour which lasted from January until May.

POST-WAR CHANGE

PRE-WAR and post-war Glyndebourne were bound to be as different as the pre-war and post-war world. While still a rich man, John Christie was no longer very rich. He had sold the Glyndebourne cellar of German wine for £17,000. Yet he offered £100,000 for the freehold of the Royal Opera House, Covent Garden, but he was unable to proceed 'owing to the hostility which existed in certain quarters', led by John Maynard Keynes. Eventually Glyndebourne re-opened on 12 July 1946 with the first of fourteen performances of Benjamin Britten's new opera *The Rape of Lucretia*, produced by a team that subsequently became the English Opera Group. There were two casts, the first conducted by Ernest Ansermet, with Kathleen Ferrier as Lucretia, the second by Reginald Goodall (who had conducted Britten's *Peter Grimes* at its historic 1945 première), with Nancy Evans as Lucretia. The opera was received respectfully. Christie disliked it and was enraged when he was faced with a bill substantially larger than budget after the production had subsequently been taken out on tour. He also disliked Britten's lifestyle. But he sanctioned the revival of *Lucretia* in 1947 with Ferrier. This short season also included the world première by the English Opera Group of Britten's new comedy *Albert Herring*, set in a village greengrocer's and with caricatures of the worthies of a small town. Christie greeted members of the audience with the words, 'This isn't our sort of thing, you know'. There were to be no more Britten operas at Glyndebourne until 1981. Ferrier also sang the title role in Gluck's *Orfeo*, sung in Italian and directed by Carl Ebert, back from Turkey. The conductor was Fritz Stiedry. A recording preserves Ferrier's hypnotic performance.

The period from 1947 to 1950 presented Glyndebourne with a considerable challenge. There was no money and future funding would have to come from the state (an anathema to Christie) or perhaps a new Glyndebourne could be started in North America. However, back in 1940, when *The Beggar's Opera* was taken to Edinburgh, Audrey had said to Bing: 'What a place for a festival!'. In 1945 Bing proposed the idea to the Lord Provost, offering Glyndebourne's help and advice but not its money. So in

Opposite:
Members of the
audience arriving
at Glyndebourne
by coach from
Lewes station,
1958.

Tarquinius contemplates Lucretia's chaste beauty. Otakar Kraus and Kathleen Ferrier in the roles, 1946.

Glyndebourne took over the management of The Children's Theatre between 1945 and 1950. The company toured plays, with adult casts, all around the country, and gave over one thousand performances, which were seen by more than half-a-million children.

The Children's Theatre

under the Management of GLYNDEBOURNE *in association with* TOYNBEE HALL
All enquiries to the Secretary
THE CHILDREN'S THEATRE Ltd., 23 BAKER STREET, LONDON, W.1

1947 the first Edinburgh International Festival was launched and in August Ebert and Bing, with Bing's new assistant Moran Caplat, a former naval officer, took the pre-war productions of *Macbeth* and *Figaro* to Edinburgh. Margherita Grandi returned as Lady Macbeth and the non-singing role of Fleance was taken by twelve-year-old George Christie. For the 1948 Edinburgh Festival, Ebert revived *Don Giovanni*. Paolo Silveri sang the title role and Ljuba Welitsch was Donna Anna. As Don Ottavio, Richard Lewis began his long association with Glyndebourne. There was a new production by Ebert of *Così fan tutte*. The conductor was another name which will recur often, Vittorio Gui. In the 1949 *Così*, Sena Jurinac, one of the 'goddesses' who were to dominate Glyndebourne for the next sixty years, sang Dorabella. The other Ebert production was of Verdi's *Un ballo in maschera*.

None of these riches was seen at Glyndebourne. After the 1947 season the only music performed in the theatre was a series of concerts, some by the Royal Philharmonic Orchestra under Beecham. The 'happy atmosphere of pre-war days', to quote Bing, had evaporated. Audrey was not well and Fritz Busch was out of favour with the Christies since he had passed over Audrey, when she badly needed money, when he was casting Susanna for the Metropolitan Opera, New York, in 1943. But in 1949 Bing left to become General Manager of the Met and was succeeded at Glyndebourne by Moran Caplat. When there seemed to be a chance of a 1950 Glyndebourne season, Caplat persuaded John Christie to bury hatchets and invite Busch, who agreed at once. The optimism for 1950 arose from plans for the 1951 nationwide Festival of Britain. The Treasury voted, for the first and only time, a large sum to enable Glyndebourne to stage four Mozart operas, but it was available only for 1951. Caplat's suggestion that two operas should be done in 1950, with another two the following year, was vetoed, but he went to see Glyndebourne's friend, John Spedan Lewis of the John Lewis Partnership, who came up with a £12,000 guarantee against loss for 1950. Fourteen performances were given in July of *Die Entführung* and *Così fan tutte*. In the latter, Jurinac now sang Fiordiligi (to rapturous applause). Glyndebourne was back.

Poster for the Glyndebourne Opera performances at the first Edinburgh Festival, 1947.

Victoria station had its afternoon passengers in evening dress again; the gardens were back to pre-war glories, the audience strolled on the lawns; in spite of petrol rationing the cars and (perhaps fewer) chauffeurs returned; and in each of the dressing-rooms on first nights was a half-bottle of 'Mrs Christie's champagne'. A combination of Spedan Lewis's support and Busch's return had helped to re-animate the place.

An Osbert Lancaster cartoon used in the Festival programme book, 1957.

29

A month later Glyndebourne took its *Figaro* to Edinburgh. But the major attraction was the nine performances of Richard Strauss's first version of *Ariadne auf Naxos*. Décor was by Oliver Messel and Beecham conducted. In the Molière play that forms the first part, the veteran actor Miles Malleson played Monsieur Jourdain, and in the opera Hilde Zadek and Peter Anders were Ariadne and Bacchus. This version was not performed at Glyndebourne until 1962. The 1951 Festival opened with the first professional performance in England of Mozart's *Idomeneo* in the edition prepared for Busch by Hans Gal. Busch's conducting, Ebert's direction, and Messel's sets and costumes set a new standard: Richard Lewis was a marvellous Idomeneo, Jurinac an Ilia still thought to be unsurpassed, Léopold Simoneau a tenor Idamante, though Birgit Nilsson as Elettra made less impact than had been expected. The three other Mozart operas were *Don Giovanni* (designed by John Piper), *Così fan tutte,* in which Sesto Bruscantini made his Glyndebourne debut, and *Figaro,* with Lisa Della Casa as the Countess. A performance of *Così* was televised by the BBC. There had been press criticism of Busch's conducting and it was ominous when he was taken ill one evening and could not continue after Act 1 of *Don Giovanni.*

Cover design by Oliver Messel for the very first Glyndebourne Festival programme book to cover the whole season. It was inspired by a similar idea used at the Aix-en-Provence Festival.

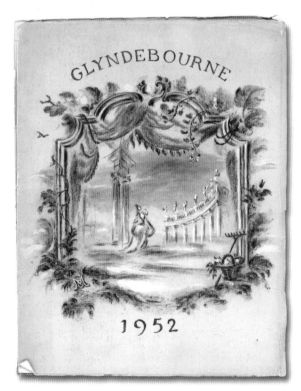

John Pritchard was driven at speed from Eastbourne, where he was bathing, and took over for the rest of the season. At Edinburgh the fiftieth anniversary of Verdi's death was marked by nine uncut performances of *La forza del destino* (without an Italian in the cast), all conducted by Busch, who shared the nine performances of *Don Giovanni* with Pritchard. The final performance was on 9 September. Five days later, in the Savoy Hotel, London, Busch died from a heart attack. His integrity, energy and sense of humour, and his belief that the heart of the performance comes from the pit, were the chief features of all that he brought to Glyndebourne.

Something still had to be done about finance, so at the end of the year the Glyndebourne Festival

Society was founded to raise £25,000 a year. Among the 'perks' for members (806 at the start) were priority booking for a limited number of tickets per season and a free copy of the lavishly produced programme book, which was the brainchild of N. T. (Miki) Sekers, the Hungarian-born founder of West Cumberland Silk Mills and a passionate patron of music. Sekers's aim was to persuade forty firms to pay £500 a page in the programme, thus providing another £20,000. Even so, John Christie had to meet a deficit of nearly £18,000 on the 1952 season.

Designer Osbert Lancaster making adjustments to the beard worn by Nan Merriman as Baba the Turk in Stravinsky's *The Rake's Progress* at the Edinburgh Festival, 1953.

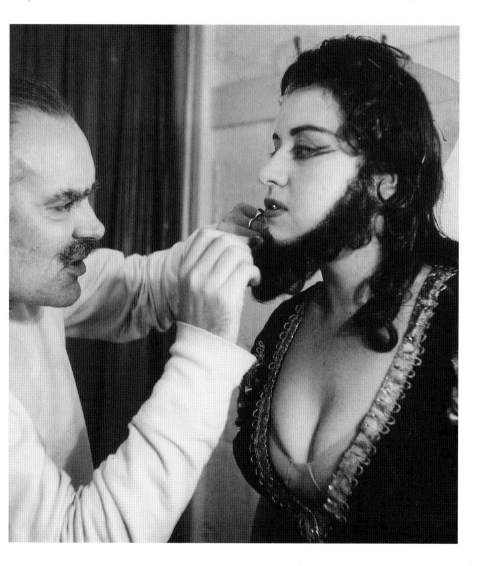

Three of the four operas that season were conduced by Vittorio Gui. *Macbeth* was revived. Glyndebourne's first Rossini, designed by Messel, sparkled, with Marina de Gabarain in the title role of *La Cenerentola*. Then there was the almost obligatory *Così* revival. There was no visit to Edinburgh this year, the Festival having invited the Hamburg Opera instead. There was loud Scottish protest.

On 31 May 1953, two days before the coronation of Elizabeth II, Audrey Christie died. Her last wish was that the season should open as planned. Three operas were added to the repertory. In Gluck's *Alceste* Magda László sang the title role, and Messel designed the revised (1916) version of Strauss's *Ariadne auf Naxos* in which the play is replaced by a short and brilliant sung Prologue. Jurinac sang the young Composer, one of her most compelling roles. On the afternoon of 19 June, before the evening performance of *Alceste,* Sesto Bruscantini (Don Alfonso) and Sena Jurinac (Fiordiligi) went into Lewes to be married. (Alas, it did not last.) The third novelty was reserved for Edinburgh, the first stage performance in Britain of Stravinsky's *The Rake's Progress*, produced by Ebert and designed by Osbert Lancaster.

In the New Year Honours List in 1954, John Christie was made a Companion of Honour. He had refused a knighthood some years earlier. Another honour that came his way at this time was from the German government and was presented to him during a dinner interval. As he and the Ambassador entered the foyer afterwards, they were greeted by Sock the pug. John removed the red silk collar from his neck and put it round the dog's saying, 'Sock, I think you deserve this as much as I do'. The Strauss and Stravinsky operas were in Glyndebourne's 1954 season with cast changes: as Sellem the auctioneer in *The Rake,* Hugues Cuénod made the first of many Glyndebourne appearances. As a curtain-raiser to *Ariadne,* Busoni's amusing one-act *Arlecchino* had its first British stage production. *Don Giovanni* was conducted by Georg Solti, but this conjunction did not work and was never repeated.

In 1954, the Glyndebourne Arts Trust was formed. It took over from John Christie the lease of all the principal buildings and one hundred acres of the estate for sixty-six years less a day at a peppercorn rent and also guaranteed continuation of the opera. It was agreed that 'Mr Christie and his colleagues shall continue to be responsible for its direction and administration'. For its part, the Trust would co-operate with Glyndebourne Productions Ltd., which would prepare the artistic and financial programme for each season and submit an annual budget for the Trust's approval.

Rossini's hilarious Crusades comedy *Le Comte Ory* was in the 1955 Glyndebourne season and the last visit to Edinburgh

included Verdi's *Falstaff*, an opera made for Glyndebourne, with Fernando Corena as Sir John, sets by Osbert Lancaster, and with Carlo Maria Giulini conducting. It was a triumph, but Glyndebourne did not see it until 1957 because 1956 was the bicentenary of Mozart's birth and forty-eight performances of six of his operas were staged. There were new Messel sets for *Die Entführung* and *Die Zauberflöte*. Jurinac's Fiordiligi and Donna Anna were heard at Glyndebourne for the last time. A short visit to Liverpool in September included a *Figaro* in which Joan Sutherland sang the Countess. She had shared the role with Elisabeth Grümmer in the summer. Among the highlights of the 1957 season, the Composer in *Ariadne* was sung by the Swedish soprano Elisabeth Söderström. The following year the company went to Paris in May with *Le Comte Ory* and *Falstaff*, and then gave fifty-one performances of seven operas at the Festival in Sussex. The major off-stage event was the marriage of George Christie to Mary Nicholson in August. Mary was the perfect choice to follow Audrey as hostess, gardens supremo and enchantress. A little later George succeeded his father as chairman of Glyndebourne Productions. A new regime was forming in time for the twenty-fifth anniversary of the opening of the theatre.

The 1959 season was extended to the middle of August with sixty-eight performances. It opened with Strauss's *Der Rosenkavalier* produced by Ebert, with sets by Messel. Leopold Ludwig conducted a reduced orchestration, said to have been approved by Strauss for Busch. The Marschallin was sung by Régine Crespin, Octavian by Söderström (who was also the new Susanna and was rapidly assuming Glyndebourne goddess status after Jurinac) and Sophie by Anneliese Rothenberger. The other new production, by one of the European leading lights, Günther Rennert, was of *Fidelio* with Vittorio Gui conducting, with huge sensitivity and dramatic flow, Beethoven's one and only opera. The season ended on a sad note with the retirement of Carl Ebert, at the age of seventy-two, as Artistic Director. He had served for nineteen seasons and had produced twenty different operas. He was generally regarded as better in tragedy, but his influence, through Glyndebourne, on opera production in Britain was immense.

Opposite: Elisabeth Söderström as Octavian dressed as the maid, Mariandl, in *Der Rosenkavalier*, 1959.

The silver rose, designed by Oliver Messel and made by the Glyndebourne Props Department for *Der Rosenkavalier*, 1959.

GEORGE AND MARY

WITH THE gradual disappearance of the 'old guard', George Christie's task was to find new blood to keep Glyndebourne enterprising but not to alienate its audiences and change its atmosphere. The 1960s found Glyndebourne at its lowest ebb and was a decade of slow change. George was very conscious that Glyndebourne was regarded as 'elitist' – 'that boring old refrain', he said – and the highbrow playground of the wealthy and privileged. In many ways this was inevitable. It was not easily accessible; picnics and good wines and evening dress were socially divisive and the operas were sung in foreign languages. But opera at its best was what Glyndebourne was about – and no one could say, as they did of Covent Garden, that Glyndebourne's pleasures for the few were provided by money from taxpayers who never went near opera. George and Mary were subtly creating their own Glyndebourne without jettisoning the best of the old, but it took time. Their own family, too, was to grow during the 1960s. Hector was born in 1961, Gus in 1963 and Louise in 1966. Ptolemy arrived in 1971. Mary's charm, tact and care for the gardens more and more resembled Audrey's.

Bellini's *I Puritani* was added to the repertory in 1960 as a vehicle for Joan Sutherland and to introduce a new producer in Franco Enriquez. Together with *Falstaff*, it was taken to Edinburgh at the end of the season, a one-off return to the Festival. Beecham was to have conducted *Die Zauberflöte* but was ill and his place was taken by Colin Davis. The new Zerlina in *Don Giovanni* in 1961 was Mirella Freni. In 1961 the première of Hans Werner Henze's *Elegy for Young Lovers* was staged, to a libretto by W. H. Auden and Chester Kallman. It was not the happiest of times. In the cast was Söderström, who said that the opera was known by some as 'Allergy for Young Buggers'. Henze overheard one member of the audience say to another, 'We must warn poor Gwendoline'. Auden and Rennert were at daggers drawn. More expansion of the repertory came in 1962 with Debussy's *Pelléas et Mélisande* in Beni Montresor's beautiful sets and Monteverdi's *L'incoronazione di Poppea* in Raymond Leppard's edition, which led the revival of baroque opera. In 1963 the last opera by Richard Strauss,

Opposite:
Janet Baker as
Dido in *Dido and
Aeneas*, 1966.

John Christie outside the front of Glyndebourne house with his daughter Rosamond, daughter-in-law Mary, son George, and pugs Sock and Vino.

Capriccio, proved to be a made-for-Glyndebourne piece in Rennert's production with Söderström as the Countess. New and distinguished names in the casts in these years included Gundula Janowitz and Luciano Pavarotti (Ilia and Idamante in *Idomeneo* 1964), Margaret Price and Josephine Veasey. A former member of the chorus, Janet Baker, sang Purcell's Dido in a BBC Television film made at Glyndebourne in 1965 and then sang the role in the 1966 season. Donizetti's *Anna Bolena*, Rossini's *La pietra del paragone*, Handel's *Jephtha*, Glyndebourne's first Puccini (*La bohème*), and another Leppard baroque success, Cavalli's *L'Ormindo*, added spice to the repertory. Tchaikovsky's *Eugene Onegin* in 1968 was memorable for Söderström's Tatyana. Many of these productions were conducted by John Pritchard, who was appointed Music Director in 1963. The London Philharmonic replaced the RPO as orchestra-in-residence for the summer from 1964, sharing the honours with the Orchestra of the Age of Enlightenment from 1989 (they were made Associate Orchestra in 2002).

Glyndebourne during the late 1960s was facing stronger competition from Covent Garden, Sadler's Wells (soon to be English National Opera) and the regional companies. George Christie wanted to find a way of extending

Glyndebourne's influence by providing opportunities for the many excellent young singers in the chorus to take on major roles and to offer Glyndebourne standards to a wider audience. So in 1968 he launched Glyndebourne Touring Opera with Brian Dickie as its administrator and Myer Fredman as principal conductor. The first season, consisting of *Don Giovanni*, *L'Ormindo*, *L'elisir d'amore* and *The Magic Flute*, toured for six weeks in the regions. The Northern Sinfonia was the first orchestra, followed later by the Bournemouth Sinfonietta and the London Sinfonietta until in 1989, GTO formed its own orchestra. Subsidy was essential and came from the Gulbenkian Foundation and the Arts Council. After four years, the period of the tour was moved from the spring to the autumn. It became not unusual

John Pritchard conducting a rehearsal in the Ebert Room, with John Cox seated behind.

On-stage rehearsal for *Le nozze di Figaro*, 1962. Edith Mathis as Cherubino (seated), producer Carl Ebert, Mirella Freni as Susanna, and Carlo Cava as Dr Bartolo.

The Royal Court Theatre Liverpool **Playbill** PROGRAMME 1ˢ

Programme from the Royal Court Theatre, Liverpool, one of the venues for Glyndebourne Touring Opera's season, 1969.

for some of the touring casts to be considered better than those who had performed in the summer.

There was no question of seeking subsidy for the main Festival. Relying on box-office receipts to cover eighty per cent of costs was no longer feasible at a time of rising inflation, so George Christie formed a finance committee to raise money from industry and private individuals. The results were spectacular.

The 1970s was a vintage decade. Singers, conductors, producers and designers surpassed even Glyndebourne's standards and set a new benchmark. The producer John Cox had worked with Ebert but made his individual mark in 1971 with *Ariadne auf Naxos*. The following year he was appointed Director of Productions. He was joined by Peter Hall, who had immense success with two of Raymond Leppard's resurrections, Cavalli's *La Calisto* and Monteverdi's *Il ritorno d'Ulisse in patria* in both of which Janet Baker attained Glyndebourne goddess status. The stage effects and the flying in *Ulisse* would have delighted John Christie. The new *Rake's Progress* in 1975 was designed by David Hockney, and continues to entrance audiences today. New additions to the repertory included Tchaikovsky's *The Queen of Spades*, Nicholas Maw's *The Rising of the Moon* (Glyndebourne's first commission and Colin Graham's only Glyndebourne production), Gottfried von Einem's *The Visit of the Old Lady* (its English première), Haydn's *La fedeltà premiata,* and Janáček's *The Cunning Little Vixen,* produced by Jonathan Miller. Three Strauss operas were triumphs for Cox – *Capriccio,* updated to the 1920s, and the peepshow into the Strauss marriage, *Intermezzo* (sensibly sung in English), both star turns

Looking up from the stage into the flies during a rehearsal for *Il ritorno d'Ulisse in patria*, 1972. Anne Howells as the goddess Minerva on her flying cloud.

for Söderström, followed by the Ben Jonson comedy *Die schweigsame Frau*. Important new names appeared in 1975 and 1976. Bernard Haitink conducted *The Rake's Progress* and *Pelléas et Mélisande*, Andrew Davis conducted *Onegin*, Simon Rattle conducted *The Cunning Little Vixen*, Jean-Pierre Ponnelle produced and designed a new *Falstaff*, and Hockney designed *Die Zauberflöte*. Hall's *Nozze di Figaro*, *Don Giovanni* and *Così fan tutte* remain benchmarks and his human and domestic *Fidelio* showed another aspect of Söderström's artistry.

Dinner cartoon by Mel Calman.

41

GLYNDEBOURNE
Festival Opera

Founded in 1934 by Audrey and John Christie
General Director Anthony Whitworth-Jones   Musical Director Andrew Davis

21 MAY - 23 AUGUST 1991

LE NOZZE DI FIGARO	LA CLEMENZA DI TITO
COSÌ FAN TUTTE	THE MAGIC FLUTE
IDOMENEO	DON GIOVANNI

The London Philharmonic
The Orchestra of the Age of Enlightenment
The Glyndebourne Chorus

Glyndebourne   Lewes   Sussex
Box Office Ringmer (0273) 541111

Silhouette of Mozart © Oliver Messel 1956   Designed by Valerie Sargent   Printed by The Westerham Press England

HAITINK AND DAVIS

IN SEPTEMBER 1978 the much-loved Jani Strasser died, severing another link with the first years. The 1980s were to be a decade of change, too. Moran Caplat retired in 1981 and was succeeded as General Administrator by Brian Dickie. John Cox left to run Scottish Opera in 1981 and was not replaced as Director of Productions until 1993 by Graham Vick, but in the meantime Peter Hall had the grander title of Artistic Director. Stalwarts on the music staff such as Martin Isepp remained. New conductors were given their chance in Sussex and with GTO, among them Stephen Barlow, Bryan Balkwill, Nicholas Braithwaite and Kenneth Montgomery. Cox produced a new *Rosenkavalier* in 1980 with designs by the eighty-seven-year-old Erté, who for no good reason (other than his immersion in Art Nouveau) moved the opera one hundred years forward. Rachel Yakar and Elizabeth Harwood shared the Marschallin, Felicity Lott was Octavian and Haitink conducted. Haitink also conducted Hall's magical and classic *A Midsummer Night's Dream* in 1981, Glyndebourne's first Britten opera for thirty-three years and one of its greatest triumphs thanks also to John Bury's set. Hall's new production of Gluck's *Orfeo* was the perfect framework for Janet Baker's retirement from the stage.

The American director Frank Corsaro had success with Prokofiev's *L'Amour des trois oranges*; and the Strauss roles in *Intermezzo* and *Capriccio* which had belonged to Söderström now passed to Felicity Lott with equal acclaim. For its fiftieth anniversary, Glyndebourne began 1984 at the National Theatre in January with seventeen performances of Oliver Knussen's new opera *Where the Wild Things Are* (which joined the Sussex repertory in 1985, as did its companion-piece *Higglety Pigglety Pop!*). The Queen visited Glyndebourne, preferring Strauss's *Arabella* to *Figaro,* and George Christie was knighted in 1984.

Opposite: Poster for the 1991 Mozart season, which re-used Oliver Messel's Mozart silhouette from the 1956 season.

Moran Caplat, George Christie and Jani Strasser together on the roof terrace at Glyndebourne in 1968.

One of the costume designs by Erté for the Marschallin in *Der Rosenkavalier*, 1980.

The actual costume, made by the Wardrobe Department for Rachel Yakar in her role as the Marschallin in 1980 and 1982.

Hall contributed two fine productions to 1985 – *Carmen*, with his wife Maria Ewing, whose Dorabella and Poppea had been rapturously praised in earlier seasons, and Britten's *Albert Herring*, returning to its birthplace after thirty-eight years to almost universal delight. But even its success dimmed in comparison with the 1986 *Porgy and Bess*, produced by Trevor Nunn, conducted by Simon Rattle, and sung by an all-black cast headed by Willard White. Standing ovations followed every performance.

The pattern of the Glyndebourne season changed in 1987 to two new productions and four revivals. Glyndebourne had launched a Verdi sequence in 1986 with *Simon Boccanegra* and followed it in 1987 with *La traviata*. Marie McLaughlin was a poignant Violetta. The revival of *Capriccio* in which Felicity Lott was glorious as the Countess was also the farewell performance of Hugues Cuénod as Monsieur Taupe, the Prompter. He had performed in almost every season between 1954 and 1977. But the big event of 1987 was the production by GTO of a new opera commissioned by the General Administrator Anthony Whitworth-Jones. This was Nigel Osborne's clumsily titled *The Electrification of the Soviet Union*, based on Pasternak's novella *The Last Summer*, produced by the

American Peter Sellars. It was taken by the company to the Berlin Festival and entered the main season in 1988. A Ravel double-bill of *L'Heure espagnole* and *L'Enfant et les sortilèges* proved popular. This was also Haitink's eleventh and last season as Music Director. He had been appointed to the same post at Covent Garden. When he began at Glyndebourne he had previously conducted only two operas. Now he was wanted in the world's opera houses. His successor was Andrew Davis. Brian Dickie left for Canada and was succeeded as General Administrator of the Festival by Whitworth-Jones whose seven years with GTO had opened up new possibilities. He was to stay until 1998 and was responsible for operas by Oliver Knussen, Jonathan Dove, Michael Tippett and Harrison Birtwistle and for engaging producers such as Nikolaus Lehnhoff, Tom Cairns, Richard Jones, Graham Vick and Deborah Warner, in addition to Sellars.

Visitors for the 1988 season saw the ravages to the garden, including the loss of all of the most eye-catching large trees, caused by the hurricane in the previous autumn. They also saw the beginning of the very successful Janáček cycle produced by Nikolaus Lehnhoff and designed by Tobias Hoheisel.

The Glyndebourne management and the cast of *Arabella* being presented to the Queen backstage after the performance: Anthony Whitworth-Jones, Her Majesty the Queen, Brian Dickie, George Christie, Bernard Haitink, Ashley Putnam, John Bröcheler and Gianna Rolandi.

Costume designs
for Porgy and Bess
by Sue Blane.

Felicity Lott as the
Countess in
Capriccio, 1998.

The title role in *Kát'a Kabanová* was sung by Nancy Gustafson and Andrew Davis conducted. When it was revived in 1990, supertitles were installed, and, notwithstanding the antipathy in some quarters, were welcomed by the majority of the audience who were baffled by Czech, German, Russian and French, not to mention Italian. The second Janáček opera was *Jenůfa* in 1989

with Roberta Alexander in the title role and Anja Silja as her stepmother. *Arabella* was revived (Felicity Lott now the latest goddess) and Simon Rattle conducted the Orchestra of the Age of Enlightenment in *Figaro*, a new but less good Peter Hall production. GTO enlarged the Britten repertory with *Death in Venice*, later to enter the Festival, as have all but three of the productions originating on Glyndebourne's Tour.

The ugly sound of booing was heard in 1990 on the first night of Peter Sellars's production of *The Magic Flute*. It was set on a Los Angeles freeway and Sellars removed all the spoken dialogue, replacing some of the text in the 1991 revival. Not only Mozartians were outraged. More serious was the resignation of Peter Hall as Artistic Director. He had had earlier minor differences, but not consulting him about the removal of the dialogue was, in his view, the last straw. Nor was there much enthusiasm for Tippett's space-age fantasy *New Year*, a co-production with Houston Opera.

The bicentenary of Mozart's death was marked in 1991 by six of his operas. Nicholas Hytner directed *La clemenza di Tito*, an opera which had never before been staged at Glyndebourne. There were revivals of *Don Giovanni, Figaro, Idomeneo* and the Sellars *Flute* (with new English dialogue); and *Così fan tutte* was set by the director Trevor Nunn and his designer Maria Bjørnson on a 1920s cruise liner. Whilst ingenious and entertaining, it underplayed the darker side of the opera.

The stately great lime trees in the garden at Glyndebourne, a much-loved shady picnic spot.

The lime trees uprooted by the hurricane of October 1987.

THE NEW THEATRE

B Y THE END of the 1980s everyone knew that 1992 would be the last season in the old theatre, it began and ended earlier than usual. Excavation had already started in 1991, and opera-goers were able to see how work was progressing. There were two new productions, Trevor Nunn's thrilling *Peter Grimes* and Graham Vick's superb *Queen of Spades*. When the curtain fell on 23 July, demolition of the old theatre began at once. With it went many memories and some felt that nothing would be quite the same again. But George Christie was unsentimental. 'My father would have done this twenty years ago.' Through the annual programme book, he had been drip-feeding a message to the audience that amounted to, in his words, 'We are going to pull down the opera house before it falls down'. He equalled, if not surpassed, his father's courage and vision in knowing that the worldwide fame of Glyndebourne could not persist in the modern world in a village-hall theatre, however miraculous its achievements there. The new theatre, he told the designers, 'can be controversial to a point that does not alienate the majority'. He wanted something that would be idiomatic in the context of its setting – neither provoking violent reactions nor being depressingly reactionary. He did not seek modernism for the sake of modernism. He was against velvet plush and gilt. He wanted something which was affordable, efficiently functional and in a style which retained some of the rustic character of the old theatre. He got what he wanted from the Michael Hopkins Partnership, and like his father he took an active part in every aspect of the construction. And he set the timetable. He would not sacrifice more than one season, it had to be ready for May 1994. He and his small team also performed wonders in raising the money from business and private sources. By 1992 over eighty per cent of the estimated cost of £33,000,000 had been collected. A gala concert in July that year, attended by the Prince of Wales, raised a further £841,457.

When the theatre was completed, the general opinion was that it was a masterpiece, with good acoustics and sightlines and excellent facilities for the public (notably air-conditioning). The job had been done on time and on

Opposite:
The framework of the fly tower is removed from the old theatre on 24 August 1992.

Lighting Manager Keith Benson turning off the lights in the old theatre for the last time.

budget and everyone involved regarded it as a happy experience. Diehards felt that some of the 'old' atmosphere had gone and of course it had. But the magic of Glyndebourne reasserted itself.

In 1992, while the opera house at Glyndebourne was being demolished, the Tour celebrated its twenty-fifth anniversary at Sadler's Wells before going on to the regional theatres.

The Glyndebourne staff pictured outside the Green Room block in 1992 before demolition of the old theatre, with the Christie family on the steps behind.

Although Glyndebourne was closed in 1993, continuity was maintained by nine concert performances of three operas at the Royal Festival Hall in London, and GTO's operas at Sadler's Wells and on tour. With seats for 1,200 and forty standing places, the new Glyndebourne theatre opened on 28 May 1994, sixty years to the day since the old theatre had opened with the same opera, *Le nozze di Figaro.* Renée Fleming sang the Countess, Gerald Finley was Figaro and Alison Hagley was Susanna. Deborah Warner's production of *Don Giovanni* generated controversy by lascivious treatment of a statue of the Madonna. Revivals of *Eugene Onegin, Peter Grimes* and *The Rake's Progress* were acclaimed. GTO gave the première of Harrison Birtwistle's *The Second Mrs Kong*, a cross-centuries romance between the gorilla King Kong and Vermeer's *Girl with a Pearl Earring,* as part of its autumn tour.

Programme book
cover for 1993
by Peter Brookes.
The familiar view
of Glyndebourne
house and the old
theatre is seen as
a reflection to the
company's
temporary
residency on
the South Bank.

Costume design
for Ermione by
Richard Hudson.

Graham Vick was now Director of Productions and began the 1995 season with Rossini's *Ermione*, an *opera seria* not seen in Britain since 1819, with Anna Caterina Antonacci in the title role. Far too long a gap was the general verdict. Rapture greeted Lehnhoff's production of Janáček's *The Makropulos Case*, in which Anja Silja was an unforgettable Emilia Marty. 'Is there consistently better opera anywhere in the world?' one critic asked. The world could judge, too, for Glyndebourne productions were televised worldwide and its videos and DVDs were similarly marketed.

Handel at last returned to the repertory in 1996 when Sellars produced *Theodora* in a challenging, updated production

Lorraine Hunt
as Irene in
Peter Sellars's
production of
Handel's *Theodora*.

Glyndebourne's
auditorium, with
the set for *Pelléas
et Mélisande* on
stage.

which was much liked. William Christie conducted and Dawn Upshaw sang the title role. But it was Lorraine Hunt as Irene who transfixed all who heard her. Whitworth-Jones's enterprise brought in Berg's *Lulu* in its three-act version and, in 1997, Puccini's *Manon Lescaut* and Britten's problem-opera *Owen Wingrave*, which GTO had performed the previous year. Vick's experimental productions of the three Mozart/da Ponte operas began in 1998 with *Così* and there were fears that he had lost his touch when compared with Jean-Marie Villégier's silent-movie treatment of Handel's *Rodelinda*. Verdi's *Simon Boccanegra* was conducted by Mark Elder, who had worked at Glyndebourne earlier in his career. Opinions differed over Vick's single-set presentation of *Pelléas et Mélisande,* which opened the 1999 season, but not over John Tomlinson's terrifying Golaud. The Lehnhoff-Hoheisel duo staged

Gus Christie with his father George in the gardens at Glyndebourne.

a *Bartered Bride* set in Communist times. GTO contributed Jonathan Dove's *Flight* to the Festival, having premièred it on the 1997 Tour. This engaging opera was produced by Richard Jones, a controversial but never boring director. At the end of this season Whitworth-Jones left the post of General Director and was succeeded by Nicholas Snowman.

On 31 December 1999, his sixty-fifth birthday, George Christie handed over chairmanship of the board of Glyndebourne Productions to his thirty-seven-year-old son Gus, who had worked as a maker of wildlife films in Africa and the United States and for the BBC. Gus had two very hard acts to follow – his father and grandfather, autocratic democrats both, and both with more than a touch of genius. George and Mary continued to live at Glyndebourne for two more years before Gus moved in with his family.

YOUTH AT THE HELM

SNOWMAN'S period as General Director was short-lived. He left in 2000 and was replaced a year later by David Pickard, who had for seven years been Chief Executive of the Orchestra of the Age of Enlightenment and among other places had worked at Covent Garden. Andrew Davis left for Canada in 2000 after twelve vintage years as Music Director. His post went to Vladimir Jurowski, a Russian-born conductor based in Berlin. Thus Glyndebourne was being run by three men under the age of forty. Where was the Director of Productions? Graham Vick left in 2000 after the season that had included his three Mozart/da Ponte stagings. The *Don Giovanni* was disliked even more than Deborah Warner's. GTO opened 2000 with a new Birtwistle opera, *The Last Supper* (more of an oratorio), which went into the main season in 2001. In 2003 the touring company changed its name to Glyndebourne on Tour. This was a more accurate title, reflecting the company's integration into the main scheme and eliminating any suggestion that it was a 'second eleven'.

Two new 2001 productions were *Fidelio*, entrusted to Deborah Warner and conducted by Rattle, and Verdi's *Otello*, produced by Peter Hall, conducted by Richard Farnes, and still illuminated by the memory of the late Susan Chilcott's wonderful Desdemona. The classic Hall production of Britten's *A Midsummer Night's Dream* retained its magic on its first staging in the new theatre. Snowman's policy had been for more new productions (aided by the addition of a second rehearsal room, the Jerwood Studio) and 2002 saw three of them – Gluck's *Iphigénie en Aulide* (producer Christof Loy), Weber's *Euryanthe* (Richard Jones) and *Carmen* (David McVicar). The year also saw the appointment of George Christie as a Companion of Honour. Surely it is unprecedented for both father and son to be awarded this honour?

But what everyone had been waiting for came in 2003 when John Christie's dream came true: a Wagner opera – *Tristan und Isolde* – was staged at Glyndebourne by Lehnhoff with a dramatically lit single set by Roland Aeschlimann. Tristan was sung by Robert Gambill, and Isolde (her first) by Nina Stemme, who has since been in demand the world over for this role.

Opposite:
Danielle de Niese
in the title role
of Monteverdi's
*L'incoronazione di
Poppea*, 2008.

David Rendall and
Susan Chilcott
during rehearsals
for their roles
as Otello and
Desdemona, 2001.

René Pape was a moving King Marke and the conductor was Jiří Bělohlávek. It became the hottest ticket in town, (as it was in its two revivals, the second in 2009 being conducted by Jurowski), and it overshadowed the other 2003 offerings. A Sellars *Idomeneo* was conducted by Rattle, whose future wife Magdalena Kožená sang Idamante. (Several marriages have been 'brokered' by Glyndebourne!) A first foray into Viennese operetta with *Die Fledermaus* somehow misfired in spite of good ingredients. A *Bohème* borrowed from GTO 2000 was splendidly produced by McVicar and had Rolando Villazón as Rodolfo, though nobody, except at Glyndebourne, seemed to notice him at the time.

It was back to two new productions and four revivals in 2004, the newcomers being a *Zauberflöte* conducted by Vladimir Jurowski, and, if you count it as one, a double bill of Rachmaninoff's *The Miserly Knight* and Puccini's hilarious *Gianni Schicchi*. Alessando Corbelli was the Schicchi of

Tristan und Isolde in
2009, with Torsten
Kerl and Anja
Kampe in the title
roles.

one's dreams. Revivals of *Rodelinda* and *Pelléas* went down well. In 2005 Glyndebourne's new affinity with Handel was affirmed by David McVicar's brilliant and imaginative staging of *Giulio Cesare*, conducted by William Christie, with Sarah Connolly a noble Caesar, Danielle de Niese an irresistible Cleopatra and Angelika Kirchschlager as Sesto – luxury casting. It overshadowed the serious-minded Peter Hall production of *La Cenerentola*. Nicholas Hytner's production of *Così fan tutte* in 2006, conducted by Iván Fischer, provided

Brigitte Reiffenstuel's costume designs for Cleopatra and Tolomeo in Handel's *Giulio Cesare*.

Glyndebourne again with a staging worthy of this nonpareil among operas. Jurowski gave himself a hard task with Prokofiev's *Betrothal in a Monastery*. The 2007 season had two controversial offerings in Richard Jones's production of Verdi's *Macbeth* – in which the witches lived in caravans and some were Myra-Hindley look-alikes – and Katie Mitchell's staging of J. S. Bach's oratorio the

Benjamin Britten's *The Turn of the Screw* in Jonathan Kent's production.

Felicity Palmer
as Josefa Miranda,
the abbess, Nathan
Gunn as Father
Cayetano Delaura
and Allison Bell as
Sierva María in
*Love and Other
Demons*, 2008.

Ana María
Martínez as the
water nymph
Rusalka, 2009.

St Matthew Passion. More successful was Jonathan Kent's production (originally for the touring company in 2006) of Britten's *The Turn of the Screw*, a work made for Glyndebourne in almost all aspects.

For 2008 there were three new productions – *L'incoronazione di Poppea* (Danielle de Niese as Poppea and Alice Coote as Nero, conducted by Emmanuelle Haïm) and *Hänsel und Gretel*, a first for Glyndebourne, while Peter Eötvös's *Love and Other Demons* was the latest première in a long line of commissions at Glyndebourne. The revivals were *Carmen,* the ever-popular *Albert Herring* and *Eugene Onegin.* In *Herring* John Graham-Hall and Alan Opie, who had sung Albert and Sid in this production when it was new in 1985, had a high old time as the Mayor and the Vicar. For 2009, Glyndebourne's seventy-fifth anniversary, a rich, and varied programme was assembled, although John Christie would have been surprised, as were many others, that Mozart was excluded. But there has to be a limit to what can be done with Mozart operas. As Gus Christie wrote: 'Breaking new ground and extending our reach' were still governing factors. Jurowski conducted and Richard Jones produced a new *Falstaff*. Jurowski also conducted the *Tristan* revival, which had a new pair of lovers in Torsten Kerl and Anja Kampe, with Sarah Connolly as Brangäne. New to Glyndebourne were Purcell's *The Fairy Queen*, conducted by William Christie and produced by Jonathan Kent, and Dvořák's *Rusalka*, Ana María Martínez radiant in the title role. *L'elisir d'amore* directed by Annabel Arden, was first given by Glyndebourne on Tour in 2007. *Giulio Cesare* was again a smash hit. Its scintillating Cleopatra, Danielle de Niese, became Mrs Gus Christie in December 2009. A soprano is once again the châtelaine of Glyndebourne.

Gus and Danielle on their wedding day in December 2009.

COUNTING THE COST

W<small>E HAVE</small> come a long way since John Christie's proud boast in 1934 about setting international standards of opera at Glyndebourne. How could a theatre in a private country estate which operated for only a few weeks every summer hope to compete with La Scala, Covent Garden and Vienna? Yet it did and does. Right from the start, quality was the watchword. Glyndebourne embraced an international outlook. Its casts, conductors and directors were drawn from several nationalities. It offered work satisfaction, not with high salaries but with a long and thorough rehearsal period. Nothing was just 'flung' on the stage. It believed in exploring new or unfamiliar repertory. Even in the early years, *Macbeth, Idomeneo* and, come to that, *Così fan tutte* were relatively unknown and were box-office risks. Glyndebourne today is still a unique experience, but compared with seventy-five years ago its audience – even though it still dresses up and even though a small minority is there for kudos rather than for opera – is drawn from a much wider social spectrum. The people who run Glyndebourne have determinedly eliminated the 'elitist' image, except in the true meaning of 'the best'. The first move in this direction was made by George Christie with the formation of the touring company to make opera more accessible and to encourage new audiences. Performances for schools have proved popular, but as the touring company is subsidised, financial constraints have to be taken into account. Tour productions are not cut-down versions of the originals. Many young singers have launched illustrious careers on the tour, as have conductors and administrators.

The annual visit to the BBC Proms in the Albert Hall with one of the season's operas, pioneered by Glyndebourne in 1961, has been another way of introducing millions of radio listeners, besides those in the hall, to Glyndebourne's work, and there have been many televised relays. Glyndebourne introduced live opera on television, starting in 1951 with the BBC, then with Southern Television, TVS and Channel 4. Another means of showing Glyndebourne standards to a wider audience is by screening productions at cinemas throughout the country and abroad. DVDs help to

Opposite:
The cast of *Giulio Cesare* taking a bow at the end of the semi-staged Proms performance in 2005.

Young people in
the auditorium
before the
Macbeth
performance
for schools, 2007.

spread the gospel; and the archive is being raided to issue four CDs a year of old and new performances. Most of what is performed at Glyndebourne is recorded so its sound archive is invaluable and is equalled by its photographic archive. There is also the Glyndebourne website.

One of the most important of all these enterprises is Glyndebourne Education, founded in 1986. The seeds of Glyndebourne's education programme were sown as early as the 1950s when a concert performance of

An outside-
broadcast BBC
lorry set up on
the top of the
hill behind
Glyndebourne for
the first live relay
of an opera on
television – *Così
fan tutte* in 1951.

Fidelio was presented at HMP Lewes. Some twenty years later, Glyndebourne presented the first of a number of bi-annual Kent and Sussex Schools Festivals and this has now developed into an annual programme of performances for schools. But what makes Glyndebourne Education unique is its commitment to commissioning a range of community operas. In the early 1990s Glyndebourne commissioned the composer Jonathan Dove, a former assistant chorus master for GOT, to create operas for Hastings, Ashford and Peterborough. Glyndebourne's commitment to work of this kind led to later commissioned operas being performed in the main theatre. *Misper* (police-speak for missing person), by the composer John Lunn and the librettist Stephen Plaice, was such a success that it had to be repeated the next year and was followed in 2000 by *Zoë*, commissioned from the same creative team, later filmed for Channel 4. This led to a hip-hop version of *Così* called *School4Lovers* in 2006 and in 2010 to *Knight Crew*, an updating of the Arthurian legend commissioned from writer Nicky Singer and Glyndebourne's first composer-in-residence Julian Philips.

Nuala Willis as Mother Fen surrounded by a chorus made up of local Peterborough inhabitants in Glyndebourne Education's community opera *In Search of Angels*, 1995.

A new opera for young people

MISPER

GLYNDEBOURNE

27 February - 1 March 1997

Artwork for Glyndebourne Education's first children's opera, *Misper*.

One of the pleasures of browsing through Glyndebourne programme books – collector's items all – is to read through the chorus lists and discover now-famous names – Janet Baker, Susan Bullock, Kate Royal, John Tomlinson, Gerald Finley, to mention but a few. Recognising that many singers in the Glyndebourne Chorus are on the brink of international solo careers, Glyndebourne launched the Jerwood Chorus Development Scheme in 2005, offering these young artists the opportunity to develop further their talent and skills. The culmination of each year's programme is a fully staged performance in the Jerwood Studio, which in turn offers further opportunities for up-and-coming conductors and directors.

Funding for all this enterprise presents a challenge at a time of economic decline. Individuals rather than companies have now become the main source of income – seventy per cent of the total sponsorship. Some individuals support complete productions, others form a syndicate. Hiring out productions to foreign companies has proved to be helpful, and some productions have been sold. But it is still true that seventy-five per cent of Glyndebourne's costs are met by ticket sales.

Glyndebourne continues to mix new productions with revivals as demonstrated by the 2010 Festival, which added *Billy Budd* to the Britten canon, with Michael Grandage directing his first opera, and a new *Don Giovanni* directed by Jonathan Kent. Revivals of *Così fan tutte*, *Macbeth*, *Hänsel und Gretel*, and the longest-running Glyndebourne production, the 1975 John Cox-David Hockney *The Rake's Progress*, completed the first decade of the twenty-first century.

As the foregoing pages indicate, Glyndebourne has changed and progressed since 1934 but in essence remains the same. It is sometimes hard to remember that this idyllic place is the headquarters of an

Opera-goers congregating on the lawns at Glyndebourne before a performance.

international opera house with, behind the scenes, all the rivalries, quarrels and displays of temperament, as well as the camaraderie and generosity that one finds in any theatre. The view of the Downs is breathtaking; the cows and sheep graze beyond the ha-ha; the gardens are fragrant; the atmosphere is friendly and welcoming; there is the joy of reunion with friends, who include the staff at the box-office and in the restaurants. Yes, there are still the grumblers who don't want to dress up and who mutter about 'elitism', conveniently forgetting that football supporters spend far more following their team over a season than opera-lovers spend on their pastime. Away with such thoughts and away with memories of nights when the opera and/or the performance have been below standard and it has rained. Think rather of what Michael Henderson wrote in the *Daily Telegraph*: 'Many a night you don't want to leave the place. You want to stay behind until the last car has left, the last light has been extinguished ... the gardens of this country house, where visitors are welcome to set up picnics or simply wander about, make it just about the happiest place in England. It is like a dream of some ideal childhood, the one that we never had.' True, but we owe most – the operas, the music-making, the incontrovertible uniqueness of the whole Glyndebourne experience – to Audrey Christie's dinner-table remark: 'Do the thing properly.'

The new theatre in the evening light, 28 May 1994.

APPENDIX 1:

DIRECTORS OF GLYNDEBOURNE

CHAIRMAN

John Christie	1934–1959
George Christie	1959–1999
Gus Christie	2000–

MANAGER

Alfred Nightingale	Manager	1934–1935
Rudolf Bing	General Manager	1936–1949
Moran Caplat	General Manager	1949–1967
Moran Caplat	General Administrator	1968–1981
Brian Dickie	General Administrator	1982–1988
Anthony Whitworth-Jones	General Administrator	1989–1990
Anthony Whitworth-Jones	General Director	1991–1998
Nicholas Snowman	General Director	1998–2000
Gus Christie	Acting General Director	2000–2001
David Pickard	General Director	2001–

MUSIC DIRECTORS

Fritz Busch	Artistic Direction	1934–1939, 1951
Vittorio Gui	Artistic Counsellor:	
	Head of Music	1960–1963
John Pritchard	Music Counsellor	1963–1967
	Music Counsellor and	
	Principal Conductor	1968
	Music Director	1969–1977
Bernard Haitink	Music Director	1978–1988
Andrew Davis	Music Director	1989–1991
Andrew Davis	Music Director	1992–2000
Vladimir Jurowski	Music Director	2001–

ARTISTIC DIRECTORS

Carl Ebert	Artistic Direction	1934–1939
	Artistic Director	1946–1959
Günther Rennert	Artistic Counsellor:	
	Head of Production	1960–1967
Franco Enriquez	Adviser on Production	1968–1969
John Cox	Director of Production	1972–1981
Peter Hall	Artistic Director	1984–1990
Graham Vick	Director of Productions	1993–2000

APPENDIX 2:

GLYNDEBOURNE FESTIVAL OPERA

OPERAS PERFORMED 1934–2010

New productions in bold print.

Bach	*St Matthew Passion*: **2007**	Dove	*Flight*: 1999, 2005
Beethoven	*Fidelio*: **1959**, 1961, 1963, **1979**,	Dvořák	*Rusalka*: **2009**
	1981, 1993 (South Bank), **2001**,	Eötvös	*Love and Other Demons*: **2008**
	2006	Gay	*The Beggar's Opera*: **1940**
Bellini	*I Puritani*: **1960**	Gershwin	*Porgy and Bess*: **1986**, 1987
Berg	*Lulu*: **1996**	Gluck	*Orfeo ed Euridice*: **1947**, **1982**, 1989
Berlioz	*Béatrice et Bénédict*: **1993** (South		*Alceste*: **1953**, 1954, 1958
	Bank)		*Iphigénie en Aulide*: **2002**
Birtwistle	*The Second Mrs Kong*: 1995	Handel	*Jephtha*: **1966**
	The Last Supper: 2001		*Theodora*: **1996,** 1997, 2003
Bizet	*Carmen*: **1985**, 1987, **2002**, 2004,		*Rodelinda*: **1998**, 1999, 2004
	2008		*Giulio Cesare*: **2005**, 2006, 2009
Britten	*The Rape of Lucretia*: **1946** (world	J. Haydn	*La fedeltà premiata*: **1979**, 1980
	première), 1947	Henze	*Elegy for Young Lovers*: **1961**
	Albert Herring: **1947** (hosted world	Humperdinck	*Hänsel und Gretel*: **2008**, 2010
	première), **1985**, 1986, 1990, 2002,	Janáček	*The Cunning Little Vixen*: **1975**, 1977
	2008		*Kát'a Kabanová*: **1988**, 1990, 1998,
	A Midsummer Night's Dream: **1981**,		2002
	1984, 1989, 2001, 2006		*Jenůfa*: **1989**, 1992, 2000, 2004
	Peter Grimes: **1992**, 1994, 2000		*The Makropulos Case*: **1995**, 1997,
	Death in Venice: 1992		2001
	Owen Wingrave: 1997	Knussen	*Where the Wild Things Are*: **1984**
	The Turn of the Screw: 2007		(world première at the National
	Billy Budd: **2010**		Theatre), 1985
Busoni	*Arlecchino*: **1954**, 1960		*Higglety Pigglety Pop!*: 1985
Cavalli	*L'Ormindo*: **1967**, 1968, 1969	Lehár	*Die lustige Witwe*: **1993** (South Bank)
	La Calisto: **1970**, 1971, 1974	Massenet	*Werther*: **1966**, 1969
Cimarosa	*Il matrimonio segreto*: **1965**, 1967	Maw	*The Rising of the Moon*: **1970**, 1971
Debussy	*Pelléas et Mélisande*: **1962**, 1963,	Monteverdi	*L'incoronazione di Poppea*: **1962**,
	1969, 1970, **1976**, **1999**, 2004		1963, 1964, **1984**, 1986, **2008**
Donizetti	*Don Pasquale*: **1938**, 1939		*Il ritorno d'Ulisse in patria*: **1972**,
	L'elisir d'amore: **1961**, 1962, 1967,		1973, 1979
	2009	Mozart	*Le nozze di Figaro*: **1934**, 1935, 1936,
	Anna Bolena: **1965**, 1968		1937, 1938, 1939, 1947, **1950**,

1951, **1955**, 1956, 1958, 1959,
1962, 1963, 1965, **1973**, 1974,
1976, 1981, 1984, **1989**, 1991,
1994, 1997, **2000**, 2001, 2003
Così fan tutte: **1934**, 1935, 1936,
1937, 1938, 1939, **1948**, 1949,
1950, 1951, 1952, 1953, 1954,
1956, 1959, 1962, **1969**, 1971,
1975, 1976, **1978**, 1979, 1984,
1987, **1991**, 1992, 1996, **1998**,
2000, **2006**, 2007, 2010
Die Entführung aus dem Serail: **1935**,
1936, 1937, **1950**, 1953, **1956**,
1957, 1961, **1968**, **1972**, **1980**,
1983, 1988
Die Zauberflöte: **1935**, 1936, 1937,
1956, 1957, 1960, **1963**, 1964,
1966, 1970, 1973, **1978**, 1980,
1990, 1991, **2004**, 2005
Don Giovanni: **1936**, 1937, 1938,
1939, 1948, **1951**, 1954, 1955,
1956, **1960**, 1961, **1967**, 1969,
1977, 1978, 1982, 1986, 1991,
1994, 1995, **2000**, 2002, **2010**
Idomeneo: **1951**, 1952, 1953, 1956,
1959, 1964, **1974**, **1983**, 1985,
1991, **2003**
Der Schauspieldirektor: **1957**
La clemenza di Tito: **1991**, 1995, 1999

Osborne   *The Electrification of the Soviet Union*:
1988
Poulenc   *La Voix humaine*: **1960**, **1977**
Prokofiev   *L'Amour des trois oranges*: **1982**, 1983
   Betrothal in a Monastery: **2006**
Puccini   *La bohème*: **1967**, 1978, 2003
   Manon Lescaut: **1997**, 1999
   Gianni Schicchi: **2004**
Purcell   *Dido and Aeneas*: **1966**
   The Fairy Queen: **2009**
Rachmaninov   *The Miserly Knight*: **2004**
Ravel   *L'Heure espagnole*: **1966**, **1987**, 1988

L'Enfant et les sortilèges: **1987**, 1988
Rossini   *La Cenerentola*: **1952**, 1953, 1954,
1956, 1959, 1960, **1983**, 1985,
2005, 2007
   Il barbiere di Siviglia: **1954**, 1955,
1961, **1981**, 1982
   Le Comte Ory: **1954**, 1955, 1957,
1958, **1997**, 1998
   L'italiana in Algeri: **1957**
   La pietra del paragone: **1964**, 1965
   Il turco in Italia: **1970**
   Ermione: **1995**, 1996
Smetana   *The Bartered Bride*: **1999**, 2005
Strauss II, J.   *Die Fledermaus*: **2003**, 2006
Strauss, R.   *Ariadne auf Naxos*: **1950**, **1953**, 1954,
1957, 1958, 1962, **1971**, 1972, 1981
   Der Rosenkavalier: **1959**, 1960, 1965,
1980, 1982
   Capriccio: **1963**, 1964, **1973**, 1976,
1987, 1990, 1998
   Intermezzo: **1974**, 1975, 1983
   Die schweigsame Frau: **1977**, 1979
   Arabella: **1984**, 1985, 1989, 1996
Stravinsky   *The Rake's Progress*: **1953**, 1954,
1955, 1958, 1963, **1975**, 1977,
1978, 1989, 1994, 2000, 2010
Tchaikovsky   *Eugene Onegin*: **1968**, 1970, 1975,
1994, 1996, 2008
   The Queen of Spades: **1971**, **1992**,
1995
Tippett   *New Year*: **1990**
Verdi   *Macbeth*: **1938**, 1939, 1947, 1952,
1964, 1965, **1972**, **2007**, 2010
   Un ballo in maschera: **1949**
   La forza del destino: **1951**, 1955
   Falstaff: **1955**, 1957, 1958, 1960,
1976, 1977, 1980, **1988**, 1990,
2009
   Simone Boccanegra: **1986**, **1998**
   La traviata: **1987**, 1988
   Otello: **2001**, 2005

Von Einem	*The Visit of the Old Lady*: **1973**, 1974
Wagner	*Tristan und Isolde*: **2003**, 2007, 2009
Weber	*Euryanthe*: **2002**
Wolf-Ferrari	*Il segreto di Susanna*: **1958**, 1960

APPENDIX 3:

GLYNDEBOURNE TOURING OPERA
(RE-NAMED GLYNDEBOURNE ON TOUR IN 2003)

ADMINISTRATOR

Brian Dickie	1968–1980
Anthony Whitworth-Jones	1981–1988
Sarah Playfair	1989–1998
Helen McCarthy	1999–2004
David Pickard	2005–

MUSIC DIRECTOR

Myer Fredman	1968–1974
Kenneth Montgomery	1975–1976
Nicholas Braithwaite	1977–1980
Jane Glover	1982–1985
Graeme Jenkins	1986–1991
Ivor Bolton	1992–1997
Louis Langrée	1998–2002
Edward Gardner	2004–2006
Robin Ticciati	2007–2009
Jakub Hrůša	2010–

DIRECTOR OF PRODUCTIONS

John Cox	1974–1979
Guus Mostart	1980–1985
Stephen Lawless	1986–1990
Aidan Lang	1991–1998

APPENDIX 4:

GLYNDEBOURNE TOURING OPERA/ GLYNDEBOURNE ON TOUR

OPERAS PERFORMED 1968–2010

New productions in bold print.

Beethoven	*Fidelio*: 1979, 1983, 1990, 2001
Birtwistle	*The Second Mrs Kong*: **1994**
	The Last Supper: **2000**
Bizet	*Carmen*: 1985, 2002, 2008
Britten	*A Midsummer Night's Dream*: 1981, 1985
	Albert Herring: 1986, 2002, 2007
	Death in Venice: **1989**
	Owen Wingrave: **1995**
	The Turn of the Screw: **2006**
Cavalli	*L'Ormindo*: 1968
	La Calisto: 1972
Debussy	*Pelléas et Mélisande*: 1999, 2004
Donizetti	*L'elisir d'amore*: 1968, **2007**
Dove	*Flight*: **1998**
Gluck	*Orfeo ed Euridice*: 1982
Handel	*Theodora*: 1996, 2003
	Rodelinda: 1998, 2001
Haydn	*La fedeltà premiata*: 1979
Humperdinck	*Hänsel und Gretel*: 2008
Janáček	*The Cunning Little Vixen*: 1977
	Kát'a Kabanová: 1988, 1992
	Jenůfa: 1991, 2009
	The Makropulos Case: 1997
Knussen	*Where the Wild Things Are*: 1984
	Higglety Pigglety Pop!: **1984**
Lunn	*Tangier Tattoo*: **2005**
Massenet	*Werther*: 1970
Matthus	*Song of Love and Death*: **1993**
Monteverdi	*L'incoronazione di Poppea*: 2010
Mozart	*Don Giovanni*: 1968, 1970, 1977, 1982, 1986, 1993, 1995, 2000, 2010
	Die Zauberflöte: 1968, 1971, 1978, 1990, 2004, 2008
	Die Entführung aus dem Serail: 1969, 1972, 1980, 1988, 1997
	Così fan tutte: 1970, 1971, 1975, 1978, 1979, 1984, 1987, 1991, 1998, 2006, 2009
	Le nozze di Figaro: 1973, 1974, 1976, 1981, 1984, 1989, 1992, 1996, 2001, 2005
	Idomeneo: 1985, 2003
	La clemenza di Tito: 1993, 1999
Osborne	*The Electrification of the Soviet Union*: **1987**
Poulenc	*La Voix humaine*: 1977
Prokofiev	*The Love for Three Oranges*: 1983
Puccini	*La bohème*: 1972, 1973, 1980, **1991**, 1995, **2000**, 2004
Ravel	*L'Heure espagnole*: 1987
	L'Enfant et les sortilèges: 1987
Rossini	*Il turco in Italia*: 1971
	Il barbiere di Siviglia: 1982, 1989, 1994
	La Cenerentola: 1983, 2005, 2010
	Le Comte Ory: 1997
Smetana	*The Bartered Bride*: 1999
Strauss II, J.	*Die Fledermaus*: 2006
Strauss, R.	*Ariadne auf Naxos*: 1971
	Intermezzo: 1974
	Capriccio: 1976
Stravinsky	*The Rake's Progress*: 1975, 1977, 1978, 1980, 1992
Tchaikovsky	*Eugene Onegin*: 1969, 1971, 1974, 1994, 2002
Tippett	*New Year*: 1990
Verdi	*Macbeth*: 1969, 1973, 2007
	Falstaff: 1976, 1977, 1981, 20
	Simon Boccanegra: 1986
	La traviata: 1988, 1996, 2003
Weber	*Der Freischütz*: **1975**

APPENDIX 5:

THE CHRISTIE FAMILY TREE

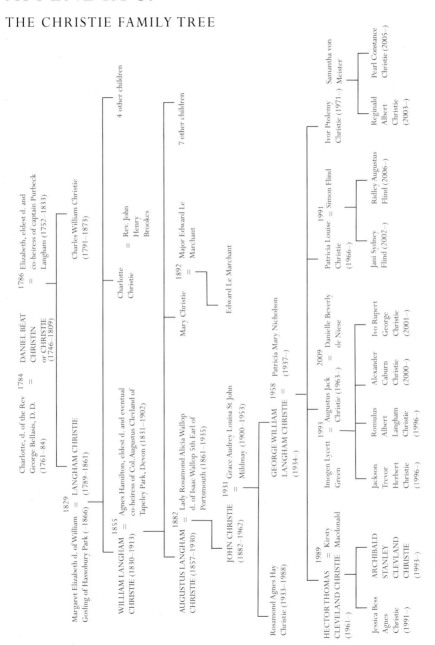

INDEX

Page numbers in italics refer to
illustrations